## Overview

The U.S. Office of Personnel Management (OPM) has prepared human resources guidance for agencies and employees on shutdown furloughs (also called emergency furloughs). A shutdown furlough occurs when there is a lapse in annual appropriations. Shutdown furloughs can occur at the beginning of a fiscal year, if no funds have been appropriated for that year, or upon expiration of a continuing resolution, if a new continuing resolution or appropriations law is not passed.

In a shutdown furlough, an affected agency would have to shut down any activities funded by annual appropriations that are not excepted by law. Typically, an agency will have very little to no lead time to plan and implement a shutdown furlough.

NOTE: This guidance applies to activities that are funded by annual appropriations. Some agency functions have alternative funding sources and, as a result, are not directly affected by a lapse in annual appropriations. Employees performing those functions will generally continue to be governed by the normal pay, leave, and other civil service rules. Agencies should consult with their legal counsel if they have further questions concerning this distinction. Employees should consult with their human resources office.

## Table of Contents

## A. General

### 1. What is a furlough?

**A.** A furlough is the placing of an employee in a temporary nonduty, nonpay status because of lack of work or funds, or other nondisciplinary reasons.

### 2. What is a shutdown furlough and why is a shutdown furlough necessary?

**A.** In the event that funds are not available through an appropriations law or continuing resolution, a "shutdown" furlough occurs. A shutdown furlough is necessary when an agency no longer has the necessary funds to operate and must shut down those activities which are not excepted pursuant to the Antideficiency Act.

## B. Employee Coverage

### 1. Who are "excepted" employees?

**A.** In the context of shutdown furloughs, the term "excepted" is used to refer to employees who are funded through annual appropriations who are nonetheless excepted from the furlough because they are performing work that, by law, may continue to be performed during a lapse in appropriations. Excepted employees include employees who are performing emergency work involving the safety of human life or the protection of property or performing certain other types of excepted work. Agency legal counsels, working with senior agency managers, determine which employees are designated to be handling "excepted" and "non-excepted" functions. See http://www.opm.gov/policy-data-oversight/pay-leave/furlough-guidance/#url=Shutdown-Furlough for copies of OMB and DOJ issuances, which provide guidance on the application of these criteria.

(Note: Presidential appointees who are not covered by the leave system in 5 U.S.C. chapter 63 are not "excepted" as discussed above. However, they are not subject to furlough because their salary is an obligation incurred by the year, without consideration of hours of duty required, so they cannot be placed in a nonduty, nonpay status.)

### 2. Are all employees who qualify as "emergency employees" for the purpose of weather emergencies considered to be "excepted employees" for the purpose of a shutdown furlough?

**A.** Not necessarily. "Emergency employees" are those employees who must report for work in emergency situations—e.g., severe weather conditions, air pollution, power failures, interruption of public transportation, and other situations in which significant numbers of employees are prevented from reporting for work or which require agencies to close all or part of their activities. Emergency employees are not automatically deemed excepted employees for purposes of shutdown furloughs. Each agency must determine which employees are excepted employees based on the law.

### 3. Who are "exempt" employees?

**A.** Employees are "exempt" from furlough if they are not affected by a lapse in appropriations. This includes employees who are not funded by annually appropriated funds. Employees performing those functions will generally continue to be governed by the normal pay, leave, and other civil service rules.

### 4. What about employees who are neither "excepted" nor "exempt"?

**A.** Employees who are funded through annual appropriations but are not designated as excepted are barred from working during a shutdown, except to perform minimal activities as necessary to execute an orderly suspension of agency operations related to non-excepted activities. These employees will be furloughed.

### 5. How will employees be notified whether they have been designated to be handling "excepted" functions or not?

**A.** Each agency will determine the method and timing of notifying employees of whether they have been designated as an excepted employee.

### 6. Why are leave-exempt Presidential appointees not subject to furlough?

**A.** Individuals appointed by the President, with or without Senate confirmation, who are not covered by the leave system in 5 U.S.C. chapter 63, or an equivalent formal leave system, are not subject to furlough. An exemption from the chapter 63 leave system may be based on 5 U.S.C. 6301(2)(x) or (xi). (See also OPM regulations at 5 CFR 630.211.) These leave-exempt Presidential appointees are not subject to furloughs because they are considered to be entitled to the pay of their offices solely by virtue of their status as an officer, rather than by virtue of the hours they work. In other words, their compensation is attached to their office, and, by necessary implication of the President's authority to appoint such employees, their service under such an appointment creates budgetary obligations without the need for additional statutory authorization. Based on opinions of the Office of Legal Counsel, Department of Justice, the Antideficiency Act prohibition on creating a budgetary obligation before an appropriation is made is not applicable if the obligation is otherwise "authorized by law." (See 31 U.S.C. 1341 and 36 Op. O.L.C. 1, April 8, 2011, at http://www.justice.gov/olc/2011/wh-offrs-exempt-from-leave.pdf.)

A leave-exempt Presidential appointee cannot be placed on nonduty status. Thus, the appointee's pay cannot be reduced based on placement in nonduty status, including via the mechanism of a furlough. As explained above, a leave-exempt Presidential appointee is entitled to the established pay of the position based on the holding of the office, not on the hours of duty.

Presidential appointees who are covered by the chapter 63 leave system are not considered to be entitled to pay based solely on their status as officers; thus, these individuals are subject to furlough in the same manner as other Federal employees. (See 5 U.S.C. 5508.) Any Presidential appointee who is a member of the Senior Executive Service (SES) or in a senior level (SL/ST) position paid under 5 U.S.C. 5376 is not exempt from the chapter 63 leave system (unless specifically designated for exemption under 5 U.S.C. 6301(2)(xi) and 5 CFR 630.211). All SES and SL/ST employees covered by the chapter 63 leave system are subject to furlough on the same basis as other employees. (The furlough of career SES members is subject to the procedures in 5 CFR 359, subpart H, and the furlough of SL/ST employees is subject to the procedures in 5 CFR 752, subpart D, or 5 CFR part 351, as applicable.)

While employees may be subject to furlough, the applicable due process procedures depend on the type of employee in question. For example, all Presidential appointees are excluded from the adverse action procedures in 5 U.S.C. chapter 75, based on 5 U.S.C. 7511(b)(1) and (3). In addition, Presidential appointees subject to Senate confirmation are excluded from reduction in force procedures, based on 5 CFR 351.202(b). If a Presidential appointee is subject to furlough but not subject to adverse action or reduction in force procedures, the agency should follow any administrative procedures required by any applicable internal personnel policies.

Note: A former career Senior Executive Service (SES) appointee who receives a Presidential appointment that would normally convey an exemption from the leave system may be eligible to elect to retain SES leave benefits under 5 U.S.C. 3392(c). If SES leave benefits are so elected, such a Presidential appointee would be subject to furlough under 5 CFR 359, subpart H.

## C. Working during Furlough

**1. May an employee volunteer to do his or her job on a nonpay basis during a shutdown furlough?**

**A.** No. Unless otherwise authorized by law, an agency may not accept the voluntary services of an employee. (See 31 U.S.C. 1342.)

**2. What happens to employees scheduled for training during a shutdown furlough?**

**A.** Employees who are neither excepted nor exempt and are scheduled for training during a shutdown furlough must be placed in a furlough status and ordered not to attend the scheduled training.

**3. May employees take other jobs while on furlough?**

**A.** While on furlough, an individual remains an employee of the Federal Government. Therefore, executive branch-wide standards of ethical conduct and rules regarding outside employment continue to apply when an individual is furloughed (specifically, the executive branch-wide standards of ethical conduct (the standards), at 5 CFR part 2635). In addition, there are specific statutes which prohibit certain outside activities, and agency-specific supplemental rules that require prior approval of, and sometimes prohibit, outside employment. Therefore, before engaging in outside employment, employees should review these regulations and then consult their agency ethics official to learn if there are any agency-specific supplemental rules governing the employee.

4. **If an employee receives a temporary appointment in another agency while furloughed, what happens to his/her benefits (e.g., retirement, health benefits, life insurance, leave)?**

**A.** Retirement, health benefits, and life insurance are handled as if the employee had actually transferred to the new agency. Leave balances are transferred as if the employee had actually transferred. (See Comptroller General opinion B-167975, September 1, 1970.)

5. **How should an agency determine the number of furlough hours for alternative work schedule (AWS) employees during a shutdown furlough? Can an employee reschedule a non-workday that occurred during the furlough?**

**A.** Employees are furloughed based on the number of hours they are scheduled to work on the days for which there is a shutdown furlough. Each agency that has an AWS program should have a policy specifying how flexible and compressed work schedules must be established and when they may be changed. Normally, such schedules are established in advance of the pay period involved. Under such a policy, an AWS non-workday scheduled to occur during a shutdown furlough should not be changed after the pay period begins.

5a. **What happens to employees on detail during a shutdown furlough?**

**A.** Detailed employees remain officially assigned to their permanent positions during the detail. During a shutdown furlough, each agency will determine the status of their employees on detail within the agency or to another agency. The home agency and the receiving agency should discuss how a detailee will be affected if a furlough is not required in the home agency but is required in the receiving agency. Detailees should not perform excepted activities at the receiving agency during a funding lapse.

6. **How are personnel working for Federal agencies under mobility agreements pursuant to the Intergovernmental Personnel Act (IPA) treated in a shutdown furlough?**

**A.** The specific authority for furloughing personnel who are working under mobility agreements pursuant to the IPA, either inside the Federal Government or with other organizations, will depend upon the nature of individual agreements, the status of the appointments, and/or the funding arrangements for the assignments. As a general rule, the following principles are applicable in determining whether to furlough personnel on IPA mobility assignments:

- Personnel from non-Federal organizations on appointments to the Federal Government are subject to furlough in the same manner as other employees.

- Personnel on detail to Federal agencies from non-Federal organizations may continue working, provided that the non-Federal organizations pay the total costs of the detail.

- Personnel on detail to Federal agencies from non-Federal organizations that share part of the costs of detail may continue to work if the Federal portion of the cost was obligated from prior appropriations at the time of the IPA mobility agreements. In the event that a furlough takes place during a time for which no funds are appropriated, the assignment should be terminated.

- Personnel on detail to Federal agencies from non-Federal organizations that do not pay or share the costs of the detail are subject to furlough in the same manner as other employees.

## D. Pay

**1. Will excepted employees be paid for performing work during a shutdown furlough? If so, when will excepted employees receive such payments?**

**A.** Agencies will incur obligations to pay for services performed by excepted employees during a lapse in appropriations, and those employees will be paid after Congress passes and the President signs a new appropriation or continuing resolution.

(Note: Presidential appointees who are not covered by the leave system in 5 U.S.C. chapter 63 are not subject to furlough, but are also barred from receiving pay during a lapse in appropriations. These Presidential appointees will be paid after Congress passes and the President signs a new appropriation or continuing resolution.)

**2. Will employees who are furloughed get paid?**

**A.** Congress will determine whether furloughed employees receive pay for the furlough period.

**3. Will employees receive a paycheck for hours worked prior to a lapse in appropriations?**

**A.** Under Office of Management and Budget (OMB) guidance issued in 1980 (below), employees will receive this paycheck. Although the payroll for the last pay period before the lapse will be processed potentially during a period of furlough, the minimum number of payroll staff necessary for this process will be excepted from furlough for the minimum time required to issue the checks, including checks for the last pay period before the lapse. This guidance can be found in OMB's August 28, 1980, Bulletin No. 80-14, Shutdown of Agency Operations Upon Failure by the Congress to Enact Appropriations, paragraph 3.b.(1) (Appropriations and funds). OMB has reviewed and concurs in this answer.

4. **When an employee's pay is insufficient to permit all deductions to be made because a shutdown furlough occurs in the middle of a pay period and the employee receives a partial paycheck, what is the order of withholding precedence?**

   **A.** Agencies will follow the guidance on the order of precedence for applying deductions from the pay of its civilian employees when gross pay is insufficient to cover all authorized deductions found at http://www.chcoc.gov/transmittals/TransmittalDetails.aspx?TransmittalID=1477.

5. **May an excepted employee be permitted to earn premium pay (e.g., overtime pay, Sunday premium pay, night pay, availability pay) during the furlough period?**

   **A.** Yes. Excepted employees who meet the conditions for overtime pay, Sunday premium pay, night pay, availability pay and other premium payments will be entitled to payment in accordance with applicable rules, subject to any relevant payment limitations. Premium pay may be earned but cannot be paid until Congress passes and the President signs a new appropriation or continuing resolution.

## E. Performance Awards and Within-Grade Increases

1. **If agency performance management policies and practices require the payment of performance awards to employees, can the payment be delayed until after the shutdown furlough?**

   **A.** Yes. Neither law nor regulation requires agencies to pay performance awards granted under 5 U.S.C. chapters 43 and 45 and 5 CFR 451.104(a)(3). If agency performance management policies and practices require the payment of performance awards, agencies may delay payment until after the furlough when funds are available.

2. **Are agencies required to pay performance awards to Senior Executive Service (SES) career appointees during a shutdown furlough?**

   **A.** No. The applicable law (5 U.S.C. 5384) and regulation (5 CFR 534.405) do not specify when an SES performance award must be paid to a career appointee, nor do they provide a basis to pay awards when no appropriated funds are available for that purpose. Therefore, if a shutdown furlough intervenes, an agency may defer payment of SES performance awards until after the furlough, when funds are available.

3. **May agencies deny or delay within-grade or step increases for General Schedule and Federal Wage System employees during a shutdown furlough?**

   **A.** It depends on how long the shutdown furlough lasts. Within-grade and step increases for General Schedule (GS) and Federal Wage System employees are awarded on the basis of length of service and individual performance. Such increases may not be denied or delayed solely because of lack of funds. However, extended periods of nonpay status (e.g., because of a furlough for lack of funds) may affect the timing of such increases. For example, a GS employee in steps 1, 2, or 3 of the grade who is furloughed an aggregate of more than 2 workweeks during the waiting period would have his or her within-grade increase delayed by at least a full pay period. (See 5 CFR 531.406(b).)

## F. Leave and Other Time Off

**1. May an employee not excepted from the furlough take previously approved paid time off (e.g., annual, sick, court, military leave, or leave for bone marrow/organ donor leave, or compensatory time off, including religious compensatory time off) during a shutdown furlough?**

**A.** No. All paid time off during a shutdown furlough period must be canceled because the requirement to furlough supersedes leave and other paid time off rights. The Antideficiency Act (31 U.S.C. 1341 et seq.) does not allow authorization of any expenditure or obligation before an appropriation is made, unless authorized by law. Paid time off creates a debt to the Government that is not authorized by the Act. Therefore, agencies are instructed that during a shutdown furlough, all paid time off must be canceled.

**2. May an excepted employee take previously approved paid time off or be granted new requests for paid time off during a shutdown furlough?**

**A.** No. When an excepted employee is not working or not performing excepted activities in compliance with the Antideficiency Act, he or she cannot be in a pay status. Excepted employees must be either performing excepted activities or furloughed during any absence from work. The furlough must be documented by a furlough notice. If an excepted employee refuses to report for work after being ordered to do so, he or she will be considered to be absent without leave (AWOL) and will be subject to any consequences that may follow from being AWOL.

**3. May an employee work during the furlough period to accumulate religious compensatory time off hours for religious observances?**

**A.** An employee who is not "excepted" may not work during the furlough period, even to accrue religious compensatory time. However, an excepted employee may work additional hours for religious purposes if the employee is performing excepted activities, though the employee may not use those hours until after the lapse in appropriations is over.

**4. If an employee is scheduled to take approved unpaid leave during a shutdown furlough, should the agency provide the employee with a furlough notice?**

**A.** It depends. If the employee is not expected to work during the furlough period (e.g., a 1-year period of leave without pay to accompany a military spouse overseas), then agencies are not required to provide the employee with a furlough notice. If, however, the employee is scheduled to return from unpaid leave to Federal service during the furlough period, the employee should be provided with a furlough notice (effective on the date of scheduled return), unless the employee is expected to be at work performing an excepted activity.

5. **If an employee is scheduled to take unpaid leave under the Family and Medical Leave Act (FMLA) during a shutdown furlough, should the agency provide the employee with a furlough notice?**

   **A.** It depends. If the employee is not expected to work during the furlough period (e.g., an employee who has just given birth and has requested 12 weeks of unpaid leave (leave without pay (LWOP)) under the FMLA), the agency is not required to provide the employee with a furlough notice. If, however, the employee is scheduled to return from LWOP to Federal service during the furlough period, the employee should be provided with a furlough notice (effective on the date of scheduled return), unless the employee is expected to be at work performing an excepted activity. An employee on LWOP under FMLA during a shutdown furlough may not later substitute paid time off for the days of LWOP.

6. **Does LWOP under FMLA that is scheduled to be taken during a shutdown furlough period count toward the employee's 12-week FMLA leave entitlement?**

   **A.** No.

7. **If an employee is scheduled to take paid leave or other paid time off under FMLA during a shutdown furlough, should the employee be furloughed?**

   **A.** Yes. An employee must be placed in furlough status during any paid time off scheduled to be taken during a lapse in appropriations. If an employee is scheduled to take paid time off under FMLA during a shutdown furlough (either continuously or intermittently), the paid time off must be canceled and the employee must be furloughed for any period during which paid time off was scheduled. Thus, any days of scheduled paid time off are documented as furlough days. Any previously scheduled days of unpaid leave under FMLA will continue to be documented as LWOP. No days associated with a shutdown furlough period will be counted against an employee's 12-week FMLA leave entitlement.

8. **Are employees who are not excepted from the furlough allowed to take paid leave or other paid time off during periods when other employees are performing work necessary for an orderly suspension of agency operations?**

   **A.** No. All paid leave or other paid time off is cancelled during a period when a lapse in appropriations is in effect. There is no authority to obligate funds for paid time off during a lapse in appropriations. Employees who are not excepted from the furlough are allowed to perform minimal activities as necessary to execute an orderly suspension of agency operations related to non-excepted activities. Being on paid leave is not an activity necessary to execute an orderly suspension of agency operations. Agencies should determine on a case-by-case basis whether it is necessary to require employees who had been scheduled to take paid time off to report to duty to perform orderly suspension activities.

9. **May an excepted employee be permitted to earn compensatory time off and credit hours (under flexible work schedules) during the shutdown period?**

   **A.** Yes. With agency approval, excepted employees may earn compensatory time off and/or credit hours subject to requirements found in 5 U.S.C. 5543 and 6120–6133; 5 CFR 550.114, 551.531, and part 610, subpart D; or other applicable authority. Each agency is responsible for approving the number of hours an excepted employee can work related to the performance of excepted activities. Employees will not be permitted to use earned compensatory time off or credit hours during the shutdown period.

10. **If an employee has properly scheduled "use-or-lose" annual leave before the start of the third biweekly pay period prior to the end of the leave year, but is unable to use some or all of the scheduled leave because of the furlough, does the furlough constitute an "exigency of the public business" that would permit an agency to restore the leave after the beginning of the new leave year?**

    **A.** Employees in this situation should make every effort to reschedule "use-or-lose" annual leave for use before the end of the current leave year. However, if this is not possible due to a lapse in appropriations, agency heads (or their designees) are encouraged to use their discretionary authority to restore any lost annual leave by determining that the employee was prevented from using his or her leave because of an exigency of the public business—namely, the need to furlough employees because of the lapse in appropriations.

11. **If an employee has properly scheduled use of "restored annual leave" that is due to expire at the end of the leave year (because it is the end of the 2-year restoration period) but that leave is canceled and lost due to lapse of appropriations, may the employing agency restore that leave again?**

    **A.** Unfortunately, no—unless Congress enacts legislation providing otherwise. There is nothing in existing law or regulation that allows restored annual leave to be restored a second time. In fact, the Comptroller General has determined that unused restored annual leave may not be restored after expiration of the 2-year period. (See B-188993, December 12, 1977.)

12. **Does a shutdown furlough affect the accrual of annual leave and sick leave?**

    **A.** If an employee is furloughed (i.e., placed in nonpay status) for part of a biweekly pay period, the employee's leave accrual will generally not be affected for that pay period.

    However, the accumulation of nonpay status hours during a leave year can affect the accrual of annual leave and sick leave over a period of time. (See 5 CFR 630.208 and Notes 1 and 2 below.) For example, when a full-time employee with an 80-hour biweekly tour of duty accumulates a total of 80 hours of nonpay status from the beginning of the leave year (either in one pay period, or over the course of several pay periods), the employee will not earn annual and sick leave in the pay period in which that 80-hour accumulation is reached. If the employee again accumulates 80 hours of nonpay status, he or she will again not earn leave in the pay period in which that new 80-hour total is reached. At the end of the leave year, any accumulation of nonpay status hours of less than 80 hours is zeroed out so that the accumulation of nonpay status hours for the next leave year starts at zero.

For part-time employees, the rule blocking accrual of leave based on the accumulation of nonpay status hours (5 CFR 630.208) does not apply. Instead, leave accrual for part-time employees is prorated based on hours in a pay status in each pay period; thus, time in nonpay status reduces leave accrual in each pay period containing such time (5 CFR 630.303 and 5 U.S.C. 6307).

Also, please see OPM's fact sheet on the Effect of Extended Leave Without Pay (LWOP) (or Other Nonpay Status) on Federal Benefits and Programs, which has a section entitled, "Accrual of annual and sick leave."

Note 1: The term "nonpay status" refers to period during which an employee is absent from his or her tour of duty established for leave usage purposes and receives no pay for such absence. Furlough is one type of nonpay status.

Note 2: The term "leave year" is defined as the period beginning on the first day of the first full biweekly pay period in a calendar year and ends on the day immediately before the first day of the first full biweekly pay period in the following calendar year. (For example, for employees on the standard biweekly payroll cycle, the 2013 leave year is January 13, 2013, through January 11, 2014.) (See fact sheet at http://www.opm.gov/policy-data-oversight/pay-leave/leave-administration/fact-sheets/leave-year-beginning-and-ending-dates/.)

Note 3: For full-time employees with an uncommon tour of duty under 5 CFR 630.210, the accumulation limit used in applying 5 CFR 630.208 is the number of hours in the uncommon tour of duty for a biweekly pay period.

## G. Holidays

1. **Will employees get paid for a holiday that occurs during a shutdown furlough?**

   **A.** No. An employee (including excepted employees) who does not work on a holiday will not receive pay for a holiday that occurs during a shutdown furlough.

2. **Can excepted employees be required to perform work on a holiday that occurs during a shutdown furlough?**

   **A.** Yes. Each agency is responsible for determining which excepted activities must be performed on a holiday in order to carry out functions related to such excepted activities. If an excepted employee refuses to report for work on a holiday after being ordered to do so, he or she can be considered absent without leave (AWOL) and will be subject to any consequences that may follow from being AWOL.

3. **What pay entitlements will accrue to an excepted employee who performs work on a holiday during a shutdown furlough?**

   **A.** The Federal Government will be obligated to pay an excepted employee who performs work on a holiday according to the normal rules governing pay for work on a holiday. For example, under 5 U.S.C. 5546(b), a covered employee would receive his or her rate of basic pay, plus holiday premium pay at a rate equal to the employee's rate of basic pay. In addition, if such an employee performs officially ordered or approved overtime work on a holiday (i.e., work in excess of his or her basic non-overtime work requirement for that day), the employee would receive overtime pay (or compensatory time off) for that work. Of course, an employee cannot receive payment for working on a holiday until an appropriations act or a continuing resolution is enacted.

## H. Benefits

1. **Will an employee continue to be covered under the Federal Employee Health Benefits (FEHB) program during a shutdown furlough if the agency is unable to make its premium payments on time?**

   **A.** Yes, the employee's FEHB coverage will continue even if an agency does not make the premium payments on time. Since the employee will be in a non-pay status, the enrollee share of the FEHB premium will accumulate and be withheld from pay upon return to pay status.

2. **What happens if an employee wants to terminate Federal Employee Health Benefits (FEHB) coverage while in a nonpay status in order to avoid the expense?**

   **A.** Unlike other types of non-pay status, employees in a non-pay status due to a lapse of appropriations (shutdown furlough) will not have the opportunity to terminate or cancel FEHB coverage. The employee will remain covered; the enrollee share of the FEHB premium will accumulate and be withheld from pay upon return to pay status.

3. **If an employee submitted a new application or a change to his/her health insurance plan (e.g. because of a Qualifying Life Event) and the paperwork was not processed by the agency because of a shutdown furlough, how would the employee seek services or coverage?**

   **A.** New enrollments or changes in enrollment due to a Qualifying Life Event do not take effect until the employee has been back in pay status for any part of the prior pay period.

4. **Would a lapse in appropriations alter the effective date of an FEHB Open Season enrollment if an enrollment request was fully processed by an agency and submitted to the health plan prior to the lapse?**

   **A.** No. The effective date would still be the first day of the first full pay period in January.

5. **What happens if agency employees responsible for processing paper SF-2809 FEHB Open Season enrollment requests are furloughed?**

   **A.** Agencies will have to determine whether those employees may continue to process the enrollment requests if a lapse in appropriations occurs. If agencies conclude that they cannot, pending enrollment requests will not be processed until those employees return to pay status.

6. **What happens if an individual makes an FEHB Open Season enrollment change but the agency did not process the request before the furlough?**

   **A.** The individual should continue to use the old health plan until he or she returns to pay status and the enrollment is processed to the new health plan.

7. **If an enrollee required healthcare after making an FEHB Open Season enrollment change that was not processed before a furlough and received coverage under the old health plan, will the new health plan be responsible for the coverage received once the furlough is over?**

   **A.** Yes.

8. **If a furlough delays processing of FEHB Open Season enrollment changes, will the enrollment be retroactive?**

   **A.** Yes. Per FEHB regulations, all Open Season enrollments and enrollment changes are effective on the first day of the first full pay period in January.

9. **If an individual's health plan is terminating participation in the FEHB Program at the end of the current benefit year, and an Open Season enrollment change has not been processed, what should the individual do in January?**

   **A.** If the individual needs services urgently, he or she should incur the expenses and file a claim with the new plan once the enrollment change has been processed.

10. **How will someone know whether his or her FEHB enrollment request was fully processed and sent to the new health plan?**

    **A.** If the individual receives an ID card, the enrollment in the new plan is effective. If an ID card is not received, the enrollment has not been processed.

11. **How will someone know if an electronic FEHB Open Season enrollment change was fully processed?**

    **A.** If an ID card is received, the enrollment in the new plan is effective. If an ID card is not received, the enrollment has not yet been processed.

**12. What happens to an individual not currently covered under the FEHB who elected to enroll during Open Season if the enrollment has not been processed and will not be processed until after the furlough?  Does this individual still have coverage with the elected plan?  If so, when?**

**A.**  Yes, such an individual would have coverage beginning on the first day of the first full pay period in January.  Expenses incurred will be reimbursed by the plan once the enrollment has been processed.  We suggest that such individuals ensure they use the plan's providers to get the maximum benefits.  For fee-for-service plans, check the health plan's website for a list of network providers.

**13. What happens to an employee's Federal Employees' Group Life Insurance (FEGLI) Program coverage if furloughed?**

**A.**  Coverage continues for 12 consecutive months in a nonpay status without cost to the employee or to the agency.  Neither the employee nor the agency incurs a debt during this period of nonpay.

**14. What happens to an employee's Flexible Spending Account (FSAFEDS) coverage if furloughed?**

**A.**  Payroll deductions will cease for any employee that does not receive pay.  The employee remains enrolled in FSAFEDS, but eligible health care claims incurred during a non-pay status will not be reimbursed until the employee returns to a pay status and allotments are successfully restarted.  The remaining allotments are recalculated over the remaining pay periods to match the participant's election amount.

Eligible dependent care expenses incurred during a non-pay status may be reimbursed up to whatever balance is in the employee's dependent care account—as long as the expense incurred during the non-pay status allows the employee (or spouse if married) to work, look for work or attend school full-time.

**15. Will the effective date of my FSAFEDS enrollment be affected?**

**A.**  No.

**16. What happens to an employee's Federal Long Term Care (FLTCIP) Program coverage if furloughed?**

**A.**  Payroll deductions will cease for any employee that does not receive pay.  Coverage will continue so long as premiums are paid.  If Long Term Care Partners does not receive payment for three consecutive pay periods, they will begin to direct bill the enrollee.  The enrollee should pay premiums directly billed to him/her on a timely basis to ensure continuation of coverage.

**17. What happens to an employee's Federal Dental and Vision (FEDVIP) Program coverage if furloughed?**

**A.** Payroll deductions will cease for any employee that does not receive pay. BENEFEDS will generate a bill to enrollees for premiums when no payment is received for two consecutive pay periods. The enrollee should pay premiums directly billed to him/her on a timely basis to ensure continuation of coverage.

**18. Will the effective date of my FEDVIP Open Season enrollment be affected?**

**A.** No.

**19. What is the effect of a shutdown furlough on Thrift Savings Plan (TSP) contributions, investments, and loans?**

**A.** Agencies and employees should refer to the TSP website or contact their agency representative for information. Agency representatives may contact the Federal Retirement Thrift Investment Board at (202) 942-1450 for additional information.

## I. Employee Assistance

**1. Are employees entitled to unemployment compensation while on furlough?**

**A.** It is possible that furloughed employees may become eligible for unemployment compensation. State unemployment compensation requirements differ. Some States require a 1-week waiting period before an individual qualifies for payments. In general, the law of the State in which an employee's last official duty station in Federal civilian service was located will be the State law that determines eligibility for unemployment insurance benefits. (See the Department of Labor website "Unemployment Compensation for Federal Employees" at http://workforcesecurity.doleta.gov/unemploy/unemcomp.asp.) Agencies or employees should submit questions to the appropriate State (or District of Columbia) office. The Department of Labor's website provides links to individual State offices at http://www.servicelocator.org/OWSLinks.asp.

**2. Can I take a TSP loan while I'm furloughed?**

**A.** Agencies and employees should refer to the TSP website or contact their agency representative for information. Agency representatives may contact the Federal Retirement Thrift Investment Board at (202) 942-1450 for additional information.

**3. What resources are available if a Federal employee needs financial assistance during a government shutdown?**

**A.** Some agency employee assistance programs (EAP) include financial consultation services. In addition, employees may want to contact their financial institution, credit union or learn about their options through the Thrift Savings Plan (www.tsp.gov).

**4. How will Federal employees access Employee Assistance Program (EAP) services in the event of a government shutdown?**

**A.** EAP services can be helpful in providing confidential counseling and coaching with experienced, licensed counselors—including legal and financial consultation. Federal employees are advised to contact their agency's EAP office to determine whether services will be available in the event of a lapse in appropriations. Many Federal agency EAPs are serviced by Federal Occupational Health (FOH), a division of HHS. Employees who know their agency uses FOH as a provider may contact their toll free EAP phone number (800) 222-0364 (TTY 888- 262-7848) to find out how to access EAP services during a lapse in appropriations.

**J. Service Credit for Various Purposes**

**1. Is furlough or leave without pay (LWOP) considered a break in service?**

**A.** No, both mean the employee is in a nonpay, nonduty status for those days/hours. However, extended furlough or LWOP may affect the calculation of creditable service for certain purposes.

**2. To what extent does nonpay status affect Federal employee benefits and programs?**

**A.** The effects of a nonpay status (which includes furlough, leave without pay, absence without leave, and suspension) on Federal employee benefits and programs vary based on

current law and regulation. For additional information, see OPM's fact sheet on the "Effect of Extended Leave Without Pay (or Other Nonpay Status) on Federal Benefits and Programs" at http://www.opm.gov/policy-data-oversight/pay-leave/leave-administration/fact-sheets/effect-of-extended-leave-without-pay-lwop-or-other-nonpay-status-on-federal-benefits-and-programs/.

**K. Federal Employees on Military Duty**

**1. Can employees who are taking military leave under 5 U.S.C. 6323 for days covered by a furlough continue to do so during a shutdown furlough?**

**A.** No. As with other types of paid leave, paid military leave must be canceled for days covered by the furlough.

For employees on active military duty, their status as Absent-Uniformed Service (formerly

Leave Without Pay-Uniformed Service (LWOP-US)) is unchanged by periods of intermittent annual or military leave, per the guidance in the <u>Frequently Asked Questions on Military Leave</u>.

2. **Will employees continue to receive a reservist differential payment (5 U.S.C. 5538) while on active duty when they are furloughed from their Federal civilian employment?**

   **A.** No. The reservist differential payments are intended to make up the difference between the employee's customary civil service compensation and his or her military pay, and they are made from the funds of the employing agency appropriated for the payment of employees' salaries. Since funds are not available for employees' salaries during a furlough, no funds may be obligated towards any type of payment for reservist differential. However, if subsequent legislation is passed reimbursing employees their civilian pay for the period of the furlough, it will be necessary for the agency to calculate any reservist differential payments that may be owed.

3. **Will there be an impact on an employee's General Schedule or Federal Wage System within-grade increase (WGI) waiting period due to an employee being in an Absent-Uniformed Service status during a shutdown furlough?**

   **A.** No. The furlough has no impact on an employee's General Schedule or Federal Wage System WGI waiting period if the employee is in an Absent-Uniformed Service status. An absence for the purpose of engaging in military service is creditable service in the computation of waiting periods for successive WGIs when the employee returns to a pay status through the exercise of a restoration right provided by law, Executive order, or regulation. See 5 CFR 531.406(c)(1)(i) and 5 CFR 532.417(c)(4).

**L. Retirement**

1. **If a shutdown furlough occurs during the 3 years of service prior to retirement, what effect will time in a furlough status have on an employee's high-3 average pay?**

   **A.** Generally there will be no effect on the high-3 average pay unless the furlough causes the employee to be in a nonpay status for more than 6 months during the calendar year.

2. **Are the retirement rules concerning the effect of a shutdown furlough the same for employees under the Civil Service Retirement System and the Federal Employees Retirement System?**

   **A.** Yes.

3. **What will happen to employees who would have retired during a shutdown furlough?**

   **A.** For employees who, on or before the requested retirement date, submitted some notice of their desire to retire, agencies should, when the lapse in appropriations ends, make the retirement effective as of the date requested. The retirement request may be informal (such as a letter requesting retirement), and can be either mailed or personally submitted to the agency. Any additional required paper work, such as the formal retirement application form, may be completed when the agency reopens. No time spent by the retiree in such actions after the effective date of the retirement may be considered as duty time, since the individual would no longer be an employee of the agency.

4. **If an employee is scheduled to retire before the end of the leave year with an annual leave balance of over the maximum leave ceiling (e.g., 240, 360, or 720 hours, as applicable) and the furlough prevents the employee's retirement from getting processed until January, does the employee lose his or her annual leave above the maximum leave ceiling?**

   **A.** No. The employee's retirement would be retroactively applied to a date prior to the end of the leave year, and the employee would receive the full amount of accumulated and accrued annual leave in a lump-sum payment.

**M. Retirement Services: Government Closure**

1. **I'm a Federal retiree. Will I still receive my monthly annuity payment during a government shutdown?**

   **A.** Yes, Federal retirees under the CSRS and FERS retirement systems will still receive their scheduled annuity payments on the first business day of the month.

2. **How can I make updates or changes to my retirement account?**

   **A.** OPM's Retirement Services is available to assist you with your retirement account. As always, you can make many of these changes online through Services Online or by calling Retirement Services at 1-888-767-6738. Due to the volume of calls, we recommend that you first use the online services site to make immediate updates and changes.

3. **How do I report the death of a family member during a government shutdown?**

   **A.** You can report the death and apply for benefits by accessing http://www.opm.gov/retirement-services/ or calling us at 1-888-767-6738. You must still apply, as you normally would, for survivor benefits after the death of an annuitant.

   If the family member was a Federal employee at the time of death, survivors must contact the agency for which the deceased worked. If the employing agency is closed, you may need to wait until after a government furlough to begin the process.

4. **I recently retired from Federal service. Will my retirement application be delayed by a government shutdown?**

**A.** If your agency or payroll center submitted your retirement application to OPM, you will begin receiving interim annuity payments while OPM retirement specialists process your application. Because OPM Retirement Services is funded by the Trust Fund it manages, OPM Retirement Services employees will still be working normal operating hours during a government furlough.

If your agency or payroll center has not yet submitted your retirement application or the application is incomplete, you will likely experience some delay as OPM must wait on other agencies to submit all of the information needed to process your retirement. Some of these agencies may not be operating during a government furlough.

5. **I applied for disability benefits. Will my application still be processed?**

   **A.** Disability, reconsideration, and appeals employees at OPM will continue working on your case. If the application requires additional information from other agencies, expect delays during a government furlough.

6. **Can I submit a Court Ordered Benefit during a government furlough?**

   **A.** Yes, OPM employees will continue working to process court ordered benefits. If the application requires additional information from other agencies, expect delays during a government furlough.

**N. Payments upon Separation from Federal Service**

1. **If there is a shutdown furlough, how does this impact a separating employee's lump-sum payment for their unused annual leave?**

   **A.** In the event of a shutdown furlough, any payments incurred by the agency for an employee's lump-sum payment will be delayed until funds are available.

2. **How are separated employees' entitlements to severance pay affected by a shutdown furlough?**

   **A.** Funds for severance pay are obligated on a day-to-day basis as the recipient accrues continuing entitlement to severance pay by not being reemployed by the Government of the United States. (Severance pay is suspended or terminated when the individual is reemployed by the Federal Government.) Severance pay is paid at the same pay period intervals as if the recipient were still employed. Any severance payment (on a payroll payday) is linked to the corresponding pay period during which the recipient accrued continuing entitlement to severance pay. If the recipient is reemployed by the Federal Government during a pay period, he or she is entitled to a prorated severance payment covering the days in the period prior to reemployment (e.g., 2/5 of one week's pay if the recipient was reemployed on the third workday of the pay period).

Thus, in the case of a shutdown furlough, accrued but unpaid severance pay represents an obligation to be paid from funds available before the lapse in appropriations occurred. Just as payroll checks for work performed prior to a lapse in appropriations can be processed as part of the orderly suspension of nonexcepted activities, severance pay checks covering days before the lapse may also be processed.

No funds may be authorized for severance payments for days during the lapse until an appropriation is enacted.

Additional information on severance pay (including eligibility criteria and payment formulas) can be found at http://www.opm.gov/policy-data-oversight/pay-leave/pay-administration/fact-sheets/severance-pay/.

## O. Benefits under the Federal Employees' Compensation Act (FECA)

**1. How is Continuation of Pay (COP) under the Federal Employees' Compensation Act affected by a Government shutdown?**

**A.** The Department of Labor's Office of Workers' Compensation Programs which administers the Federal Employees' Compensation Act (FECA) advises that, in the event of a Government shutdown, an employee who is disabled due to his or her injury is to be maintained in COP status during the shutdown unless the agency does not have monies available to pay the salary of that employee. If the agency does not have monies to pay salary during the shutdown but the agency's budget is subsequently restored in such a way as to allow for retroactive payment of salary during the shutdown period, the employee should receive COP for any period of disability that occurs within the shutdown. In the event an agency is legally unable to pay COP to an employee because of a lapse in appropriations, the employee may file a claim for regular FECA wage loss compensation for that period.

**2. Are employees who are injured while on furlough or LWOP eligible to receive workers' compensation?**

**A.** No. Workers' compensation is paid to employees only if they are injured while performing their duties. Employees on furlough or LWOP are not in a duty status for this purpose. An employee who is receiving workers' compensation payments will continue to receive workers' compensation payments during a furlough and will continue to be charged LWOP.

**Note to Section O:** Any additional questions regarding Federal workers' compensation benefits should be directed to the Division of Federal Employees' Compensation, Office of Workers' Compensation Programs, U.S. Department of Labor. See http://www.dol.gov/owcp/dfec.

## P.  Procedures

**1.  How is a shutdown furlough documented?**

**A.**  Unlike an administrative furlough, agencies should *not* prepare an SF-50, "Notification of Personnel Action" (or a List Form of Notice for a group of employees who are to be furloughed on the same day or days each pay period) at the outset of a shutdown furlough. Instead, employees will receive a shutdown furlough notice citing the reasons for the furlough because the ultimate duration of a shutdown furlough is not known by agencies at the outset of the furlough.  Once an appropriation has been signed by the President, agencies will be instructed on the appropriateness of preparing documentation consistent with Chapters 15 and 16 of *The Guide to Processing Personnel Actions*.

**2.  In the event of a shutdown furlough, can an employee be furloughed without first receiving a written notice of decision to furlough?**

**A.**  Yes.  While an employee must ultimately receive a written notice of decision to furlough, it is not required that such written notice be given prior to effecting the emergency furlough or in person.  Advance written notice (including through email) is preferable, but when prior written notice is not feasible, then any reasonable notice (e.g., telephonic, oral, personal email, or by mail promptly after the furlough) is permissible.  See Question P.2a. for providing electronic notice of a furlough action.

**2a. May employees conduct orderly shutdown activities remotely?  May an agency provide an employee electronic notice of a furlough action?**

**A.**  In many cases, orderly shutdown activities (including the distribution of furlough notices and, where necessary, the adjustment of voicemail and email messages to reflect the agency's operating status) may be conducted remotely.  Agencies that issue furlough notices should consult with their respective General Counsels to ensure each step of the process is consistent with legal requirements.  If the nature of an employee's shutdown activities are de minimis (i.e., can be completed in approximately 15 minutes) the agency does not need a telework agreement regarding such remote work.  If an agency determines it will electronically notify affected employees of a furlough action, OPM recommends that the agency include each employee's name, address, and/or e-mail address on the decision notification so that it is clear that an employee is receiving personal notification.  Agencies should also consider including in the body of the electronic correspondence, the requirement that the employee provide an email acknowledgement of receipt.  If an agency doesn't receive a requested acknowledgement of receipt of an e-mail notification, it should consider delivering a paper copy of the decision notification to the employee at his or her home address by registered mail with a return receipt requested.  Similarly, agencies must deliver hard copy furlough notices to those employees without agency email access.

Additionally, OPM recommends that agencies consider informing employees as soon as practicable whether or not an employee is subject to the furlough and provide a contact person who can answer questions related to this issue.

Finally, agencies with bargaining unit employees are reminded that they must provide notice and opportunity to bargain over negotiable procedures and appropriate arrangements to any unions representing their employees.

**2b. What are an agency's regulatory obligations in providing an appellant the Merit Systems Protection Board (MSPB) appeal information in the adverse action furlough decision notice?**

**A.** As summarized in the April 11, 2013, Federal Register (http://www.gpo.gov/fdsys/pkg/FR-2013-04-11/pdf/2013-08503.pdf) an agency must satisfy the obligation to provide a copy of the MSPB appeal form when issuing a decision notice. Providing this MSPB appeal hyperlink form electronically (https://e-appeal.mspb.gov/) will typically satisfy the requirement of ensuring that employees subject to a decision appealable to MSPB will have effective access to the MSPB regulations and appeal form. However, if the employee informs the agency that he or she lacks Internet access, the agency is required to take steps to ensure that the employee has actual access to the MSPB's regulations and the appeal form, including providing the employee with a hard copy of these documents upon the employee's request. See Sample Notice for sample decision notice language.

**3. What information should be included in the notice of decision of a shutdown furlough when no advance notice is issued?**

**A.** The notice must specify the reason for the furlough and state that the usual 30 calendar days advance notice was not possible due to the emergency requiring curtailment of agency operations. If some employees in a competitive level will not be furloughed because they are performing one of the excepted activities defined by OMB standards, OPM recommends a statement such as the following:

"If employees are being retained in your competitive level, they are required for orderly suspension of agency operations, or they are performing one of the excepted activities defined by law."

For career members (except reemployed annuitants) of the Senior Executive Service (SES), the written notice must provide the reason for the furlough; the expected duration of the furlough and the effective dates; the basis for selecting the appointee when some but not all SES appointees in a given organizational unit are being furloughed; the location where the appointee may inspect the regulations and records pertinent to the action; and, if the notice period is less than 30 calendar days, the reason for the shortened period. For an SES probationer, the notice should also explain the effect (if any) on the duration of the probationary period. See Question P.6a. below regarding noncareer, limited term, or limited emergency appointees and reemployed annuitants holding career appointments.

All notices must include a statement of applicable appeal and grievance rights. An agency must satisfy the obligation to provide a copy of the MSPB appeal form when issuing a decision notice. Providing the MSPB appeal hyperlink form electronically (https://e-appeal.mspb.gov/) will typically satisfy the requirement of ensuring that employees subject to a decision appealable to MSPB will have effective access to the MSPB regulations and appeal form. However, if the employee informs the agency that he or she lacks internet access, the agency is required to take steps to ensure that the employee has actual access to the MSPB's regulations and the appeal form including providing the employee with a hard copy of these documents upon the employee's request.

See "Sample Shutdown Furlough Decision Notice Due to Lapse of Appropriations." This sample can be used for SES and non-SES employees.

**3a. How should the decision letter for a shutdown furlough be framed if the agency has not set a specific number of furlough days?**

**A.** While it is desirable when possible to inform the affected employee of a specific number of furlough days in the decision letter, the agency needs only to set out the maximum time that may be involved, so employees have as much information as possible.

**3b. What procedural rights apply to employees who are veterans covered under 5 U.S.C. chapter 75 and 5 CFR part 752 for a shutdown furlough?**

**A.** For a shutdown furlough of a covered veteran employee, the law (5 U.S.C. 7513) gives a covered veteran employee the same procedural rights as other covered employees. Employees should consult with their agency human resources office to determine whether they are covered by 5 U.S.C. 7513 and what procedures may apply to them.

**3c. If an employee decides to challenge a shutdown furlough, from what point would the time for appeal to the Merit Systems Protection Board run?**

**A.** Employees must file an appeal within 30 days after the effective date of their first furlough day, or 30 days after the date of their receipt of the decision notice whichever is later.

**4. In addition to statutory and regulatory procedural requirements, what other forms of communication should an agency consider when implementing a shutdown furlough?**

**A.** Considering the uncertain and changing circumstances surrounding a shutdown furlough, agencies should make efforts to ensure that employees are provided with up-to-date and accurate information. If time permits before a furlough starts, this may be done through effective union-management communication, employee briefings, periodic bulletins, and newsletters. Once a furlough begins, agencies can also consider using 800 numbers and emails to home email accounts.

5. **How does the length of a shutdown furlough affect the procedures that are used to implement the furlough of employees?**

   **A.** The length of a shutdown furlough does not affect the procedures that are used.

   For most employees, shutdown furloughs lasting 30 calendar days or less (22 workdays) are covered by OPM regulations under 5 CFR part 752, adverse action procedures. Shutdown furloughs lasting 30 calendar days or less (22 workdays) for career appointees in the Senior Executive Service (except reemployed annuitants) are covered under 5 CFR part 359, subpart H. See Question P.6a. below regarding noncareer, limited term, or limited emergency appointees in the SES and reemployed annuitants holding career appointments.

   Shutdown furloughs lasting more than 30 calendar days (22 workdays) are also covered by OPM regulations under 5 CFR part 752, adverse action procedures or 5 CFR part 359, subpart H, as applicable. When the shutdown furlough goes beyond 30 days, agencies should treat it as a second shutdown furlough and issue another adverse action or furlough notice.

   NOTE: RIF furlough regulations and SES competitive furlough requirements are not applicable to emergency shutdown furloughs because the ultimate duration of an emergency shutdown furlough is unknown at the outset and is dependent entirely on Congressional action, rather than agency action. The RIF furlough regulations and SES competitive furlough requirements, on the other hand, contemplate planned, foreseeable, money-saving furloughs that, at the outset, are planned to exceed 30 days.

6. **What procedures and appeal rights are applicable for probationers, employees under temporary appointments in the competitive service, employees who are nonpreference eligible employees in the excepted service with less than 2 years of continuous service, Schedule C employees and others not covered by 5 U.S.C. chapter 75 but also affected by the shutdown furlough?**

   **A.** There are no mandatory procedures; however, agencies should ensure that all administrative procedures required by negotiated agreements or internal personnel policies are followed, subject to any exceptions to those procedures that would apply in the event of a shutdown furlough.

6a. **What procedures and appeal rights are applicable for noncareer, limited term and limited emergency employees in the SES and reemployed annuitants holding career SES appointments?**

   **A.** Noncareer, limited term, and limited emergency SES appointees and reemployed SES annuitants holding career appointments are not covered by 5 CFR part 359, subpart H, and they may be furloughed under agency designated procedures, which should include certain minimum features, e.g., whenever possible, a written notice at least 1 day before the furlough that states the reason for, duration of, and effective dates of the furlough.

7. **How do agencies implement a shutdown furlough for administrative law judges?**

   **A.** The Antideficiency Act applies to administrative law judges (ALJs). Accordingly, they should be furloughed unless they are performing functions that are not funded by annual appropriations or meet one of the Antideficiency Act's exceptions. The Merit Systems Protection Board (MSPB) has adopted procedures for implementing furloughs for ALJs, which are described in 5 CFR 1201.137–141. Those procedures, however, do not specifically address the unique issues raised by an emergency furlough necessitated by a Government shutdown. Accordingly, agencies should consult their legal counsel about how to implement a furlough of ALJs.

8. **What happens to new employees who are scheduled to report to work for the first time during a shutdown furlough?**

   **A.** By law, individuals do not become Federal employees until they report for work and are sworn in. Agencies should consider delaying the enter-on-duty date for new employees who are scheduled during a shutdown furlough.

9. **At the time of an appropriations lapse, an employee who is funded through a lapsed appropriation is on temporary duty assignment away from the employee's normal duty station. The agency notifies the employee to return to the employee's normal duty station. Can the employee elect to delay the return? If the employees decides to delay the return, and as a result the employee incurs additional travel costs, who is liable for those additional travel costs?**

   **A.** Employees who are notified to return home should do so as soon as practicable. When an employee returns promptly, the travel expenses that the employee incurs in the return are properly-incurred obligations of the agency (as part of the agency's orderly-shutdown activities), and the agency will reimburse these travel costs after appropriations are enacted and are available for that purpose. If, however, an employee elects not to return promptly and, as a result of this decision, the employee incurs additional travel expenses, those additional travel expenses are not obligations of the agency, and will not be reimbursed (instead, the employee is personally liable for the additional travel expenses); while the employee will be personally liable for the additional travel expenses, the agency will continue to incur the obligation for those travel costs that would have been incurred if the employee had returned promptly, and the agency will reimburse such "prompt return" travel costs after appropriations are enacted and are available for that purpose. Finally, in the case of those employees who are notified by their agency that they are to remain on travel, because the continuation of their travel is in direct support of an excepted agency activity, their travel expenses are properly-incurred obligations of the agency (as part of the agency carrying out an excepted activity), and the agency will reimburse the travel costs after appropriations are enacted and are available for that purpose.

10. **What happens to current Federal employees who are scheduled to transfer to a new agency during a shutdown furlough?**

**A.** Agencies should consider delaying the enter-on-duty date for employees who are scheduled to transfer to a new agency during a shutdown furlough. Such employees would remain on the rolls of their former agency until the new transfer effective date.

11. **Will the Merit Systems Protection Board (MSPB) be addressing furlough related appeals during the shutdown?**

   **A.** Please consult the MSPB website for additional information on the processing of appeals during any lapse of appropriations.

12. **If a Government shutdown occurs, how will furloughed employees be informed when it is over?**

   **A.** Employees should follow their agency procedures, including any applicable collective bargaining agreements, which may include monitoring OPM's website (www.opm.gov) and media outlets for notification that a continuing resolution or appropriation has been signed by the President.

13. **When a Government shutdown ends, when are furloughed employees expected to return work?**

   **A.** If a shutdown were to occur, guidance concerning when furloughed employees should come back to work at the conclusion of the shutdown would have to be tailored to the specific situation. In the absence of such guidance, agencies should apply a rule of reason in requiring employees to return to work as soon as possible, taking into account the disruption in the lives and routines of furloughed employees that a shutdown causes.

## Q. Labor Management Relations Implications

1. **When a lapse in appropriations requires a shutdown furlough, what is an agency's obligation to bargain?**

   **A.** The decision whether to furlough employees and which activities are excepted from a furlough are management rights that are not subject to bargaining. See 5 U.S.C. §7106(a). However, when an agency determines that a shutdown furlough is necessary, agencies have a duty to notify their exclusive representatives and, upon request, bargain over any negotiable impact and implementation proposals the union may submit, unless the matter of furloughs is already "covered by" a collective bargaining agreement.

   In the event of unforeseeable circumstances, such as sudden emergencies requiring immediate curtailment of activities due to a Government shutdown, whatever bargaining that can occur prior to taking action should occur to the extent possible before furlough actions are necessary. However, if agreement isn't reached in the time allowed, the agency should tell the union what actions it will take and offer to continue bargaining on a post implementation basis.

2. **Do agencies have an obligation to bargain before it is known whether a lapse in appropriations will occur?**

   **A.** The law requires an agency to bargain during the term of a collective bargaining agreement on negotiable union-initiated proposals concerning matters that are not expressly contained in, or otherwise covered by, the collective bargaining agreement, unless the union has waived its right to bargain about the subject matter involved. Accordingly, there may be a bargaining obligation if a union makes negotiable proposals in advance of a shutdown that address procedures and appropriate arrangements for affected employees. Agencies should evaluate the circumstances of their situation to determine whether there is a duty to bargain on union proposals concerning furlough procedures.

3. **What is the agency's obligation in responding to a union request under 5 U.S.C. 7114 seeking the agency's furlough plan and a list of excepted and nonexcepted employees?**

   **A.** An agency is required to provide data that is normally maintained, reasonably available and necessary to perform the representational duties of a union. A union requesting information must establish a particularized need for the information by articulating, with specificity, why it needs the requested information, including the uses to which the union will put the information and the connection between those uses and the union's representational responsibilities under the statute. The union must establish that the requested information is required in order for the union to adequately represent its members. An agency denying a request for information must assert and establish any countervailing anti-disclosure interests. An agency may not satisfy its burden by making conclusory or bare assertions; its burden extends beyond simply saying "no." With this in mind, agencies will have to evaluate the circumstances of their situation to determine whether they should provide the requested information.

4. **Can union officials work on "official time" during a shutdown?**

   **A.** Unless they are exempted employees, union officials cannot work on official time during a shutdown. Furloughed employees are prohibited from working on official time, because official time is a paid status, and agencies may not incur financial obligations during a lapse in appropriations. Official time is not permitted for excepted employees because they are only permitted to work on activities that are authorized under the Antideficiency Act. Official time is used for Union representational activities, which do not fall within any of the Anti-Deficiency Act's exceptions.

5. **Will union officials have access to their union offices if they are in furlough status and therefore not entitled to official time for representational activities?**

   **A.** Generally, access to facilities during a furlough may be restricted based on funding, security or other issues. Depending on agency operations, a particular facility, or portions of a facility, may be fully or partially operational.

Access to a union office during a period of furlough should not be prevented solely on the basis that a union official seeking access is not in a duty status. Access for representational purposes would be subject to each facility's requirements at the time, including provisions in collective bargaining agreements. If furloughed union officials are allowed access, it would be solely for the purpose of performing voluntary representational functions (i.e., they could not be working on official time or in any other way incurring obligations that would require subsequent agency payment).

**SAMPLE SHUTDOWN FURLOUGH DECISION NOTICE DUE TO A LAPSE OF APPROPRIATIONS**

This notice would be used for a "shutdown" furlough, where the agency no longer has the necessary funds to operate and must curtail those activities not excepted by OMB standards. In such instances there is no advance written notice proposing the action. See 5 CFR 752.404(d) and 359.806(a)).

**NOTICE**

In the absence of either a Fiscal Year (FY) [state year] appropriation, or a continuing resolution for [agency name], no further financial obligations may be incurred by [agency name], except for those related to the orderly suspension of [agency's name] operations or performance of excepted activities as defined in the Office of Management and Budget (OMB) memorandum for Heads of Executive Departments and Agencies dated November 17, 1981. Because your services are no longer needed for orderly suspension of operations and you are not engaged in one of the excepted functions, you are being placed in a furlough status effective [enter date]. This furlough, i.e., nonduty, nonpay status, is not expected to exceed 30 days. Therefore, this furlough notice expires on [enter date]. You should monitor public broadcasts and the Internet. When a continuing resolution or an FY [state year] appropriation for [agency name] is approved, you will be expected to return to work on your next regular duty day.

This action is being taken because of a sudden emergency requiring curtailment of the agency's activities; therefore, no advance notification is possible. The customary 30-day advance notice period and opportunity to answer are suspended under the provisions of 5 CFR 752.404(d)(2). The 30 day-advance notice otherwise required by 5 CFR 359.806(a) for Senior Executive Service (SES) career appointees (other than reemployed annuitants) may be shortened or waived.

If employees are being retained in your competitive level or competitive area, they are required for orderly suspension of agency operations or they are performing one of the excepted activities defined in the OMB memorandum.

During the furlough period, you will be in a nonduty, nonpay status and you may not work at your workplace or other alternative worksite unless and until recalled. You will not be permitted to work as an unpaid volunteer. Any paid leave (annual, sick, court, etc.) approved for use during the furlough period is cancelled.

Employees who have completed a probationary or trial period or 1 year of current continuous employment in the competitive service under other than a temporary appointment may appeal this action to the Merit Systems Protection Board (MSPB). Employees in the excepted service who have veterans preference may appeal to MSPB if they have completed 1 year of current continuous service in the same or similar positions as the one they now hold. Employees in the excepted service who do not have veterans preference and who are not serving a probationary or trial period under an initial appointment pending conversion to the competitive service may appeal to MSPB if they have completed 2 years of current continuous service in the same or similar positions in an Executive agency under other than a temporary appointment limited to 2 years or less.

Career SES appointees (except reemployed annuitants) who believe requirements of 5 CFR part 359, subpart H, or the agency's procedures have not been correctly applied may also appeal to MSPB.  Career SES appointees may inspect the regulations and records pertinent to this action at the following location:  [identify location and times, as appropriate].

If you have the right of appeal to MSPB and wish to appeal this action to the MSPB, you must file the appeal within 30 calendar days after the effective date of your furlough.  If you wish to file an appeal, you may obtain information about the appeals process and a copy of the appeals form from the MSPB website at http://www.mspb.gov/appeals/appeals.htm.  MSPB requires an appeal to be filed with the MSPB regional or field office serving the area where your duty station was located when the action was taken.  Based upon your duty station, the appropriate field office is [identify appropriate regional office].  MSPB also offers the option of electronic filing at https://e-appeal.mspb.gov/.  Employees have a right to representation in this matter and may be represented by an attorney or other person of their choosing.

Bargaining unit employees may grieve this action in accordance with the applicable negotiated agreement [provide citation to negotiated agreement] or may appeal to MSPB in accordance with the procedures outlined above, but not both.  To obtain information on filing a grievance under the negotiated grievance procedure, contact [name of exclusive union representative].

*[Under the Board's October 2012 regulations, notices must also include:*

*Notice of any right the employee has to file a grievance or seek corrective action under subchapters II and III of 5 U.S.C. chapter 12, including:*

*(1) Whether the election of any applicable grievance procedure will result in waiver of the employee's right to file an appeal with the Board;*

*(2) Whether both an appeal to the Board and a grievance may be filed on the same matter and, if so, the circumstances under which proceeding with one will preclude proceeding with the other, and specific notice that filing a grievance will not extend the time limit for filing an appeal with the Board;*

*(3) Whether there is any right to request Board review of a final decision on a grievance in accordance with § 1201.155 of this part; and*

*(4) The effect of any election under 5 U.S.C. 7121(g), including the effect that seeking corrective action under subchapters II and III of 5 U.S.C. chapter 12 will have on the employee's appeal rights before the Board.*

*Notice of any right the employee has to file a complaint with the Equal Employment Opportunity Commission or to grieve allegations of unlawful discrimination, consistent with the provisions of 5 U.S.C. 7121(d) and 29 CFR 1614.301 and 1614.302.]*

*[As summarized in the April 11, 2013, Federal Register (http://www.gpo.gov/fdsys/pkg/FR-2013-04-11/pdf/2013-08503.pdf) an agency must satisfy the obligation to provide a copy of the MSPB appeal form when issuing a decision notice. Providing this MSPB appeal hyperlink form electronically (https://e-appeal.mspb.gov/) will typically satisfy the requirement of ensuring that employees subject to a decision appealable to MSPB will have effective access to the MSPB regulations and appeal form. However, if the employee informs the agency that he or she lacks Internet access, the agency is required to take steps to ensure that the employee has actual access to the MSPB's regulations and the appeal form, including providing the employee with a hard copy of these documents upon the employee's request.]*

We recognize the difficult financial implications of any furlough, no matter how limited its length. We will make every effort to keep you informed as additional information regarding the agency funding level becomes available. If you have questions, contact [*contact name, phone number, and email address*]

_____ _____

Deciding Official                               Date

I acknowledge receipt of this decision.

_____ _____

Employee's signature                         Date

www.ingramcontent.com/pod-product-compliance
Lightning Source LLC
Chambersburg PA
CBHW081807280526
45789CB00008B/3033